SHAPED BY
GRACE

SHAPED BY GRACE

YOU ARE GOD'S MASTERPIECE IN THE MAKING

MAX LUCADO

THOMAS NELSON
Since 1798

NASHVILLE   DALLAS   MEXICO CITY   RIO DE JANEIRO

Published in Nashville, Tennessee, by Thomas Nelson. Thomas Nelson is a registered trademark of Thomas Nelson, Inc.

Thomas Nelson, Inc. titles may be purchased in bulk for educational, business, fund-raising, or sales promotional use. For information, please e-mail SpecialMarkets@ThomasNelson.com.

ISBN 978-0-8499-5925-7
ISBN 978-0-8499-5924-0 (with shelf-shipper)
ISBN 978-0-8499-6450-3 (shrink wrapped)

Printed in the United States of America

12 13 14 15 16 OPM 6 5 4 3 2 1

CONTENTS

CHAPTER 1

THE GRACE-SHAPED HEART

S ome years ago I underwent a heart procedure. My heartbeat had the regularity of a telegraph operator sending Morse code. Fast, fast fast. Slooooow. After several failed attempts to restore healthy rhythm with medication, my doctor decided I should have a catheter ablation. The plan went like this: a cardiologist would insert two cables in my heart via a blood vessel. One was a camera; the other was an ablation tool. To ablate is to burn. Yes, burn, cauterize, singe, brand. If all went well, the doctor, to use his coinage, would destroy the "misbehaving" parts of my heart.

As I was being wheeled into surgery, he asked if I had any final questions. (Not the best choice of words.) I tried to be witty.

"You're burning the interior of my heart, right?"

"Correct."

"You intend to kill the misbehaving cells, yes?"

"That is my plan."

"As long as you are in there, could you take your little blowtorch to some of my greed, selfishness, superiority, and guilt?"

He smiled and answered, "Sorry, that's out of my pay grade."

Indeed it was, but it's not out of God's. He is in the business of changing hearts.

We would be wrong to think this change happens overnight. But we would be equally wrong to assume change never happens at all. It may come in fits and spurts—an "aha" here, a breakthrough there. But it comes. "The grace of God that brings salvation has appeared" (Titus 2:11). The floodgates are open, and the water is out. You just never know when grace will seep in.

Could you use some?

- *You stare into the darkness.* Your husband slumbers next to you. The ceiling fan whirls above you. In fifteen minutes the alarm will sound, and the demands of the day will shoot you like a clown out of a cannon into a three-ring circus of meetings, bosses, and baseball practices. For the millionth time you'll make breakfast, schedules, and payroll . . . but for the life of you, you can't make sense of this thing called life. Its beginnings and endings. Cradles and cancers and cemeteries and questions. The why of it all keeps you awake. As he sleeps and the world waits, you stare.

- *You turn the page of your Bible and look at the words.* You might as well be gazing at a cemetery. Lifeless and stony. Nothing moves you. But you don't dare close the book, no sirree. You trudge through the daily reading in the same fashion as you soldier through the prayers, penance, and offerings. You dare not miss a deed for fear that God will erase your name.

- *You run your finger over the photo of her face.* She was only five years old when you took it. Cheeks freckled by the summer sun, hair in pigtails,

and feet in flippers. That was twenty
years ago. Your three marriages ago.
A million flight miles and e-mails
ago. Tonight she walks down the
aisle on the arm of another father.
You left your family bobbing in
the wake of your high-speed career.
Now that you have what you
wanted, you don't want it at all. Oh,
to have a second chance.

- *You listen to the preacher.* A tubby
  sort with jowls, bald dome, and
  a thick neck that hangs over his
  clerical collar. Your dad makes you
  come to church, but he can't make
  you listen. At least, that's what
  you've always muttered to yourself.
  But this morning you listen because
  the reverend speaks of a God who

loves prodigals, and you feel like the worst sort of one. You can't keep the pregnancy a secret much longer. Soon your parents will know. The preacher will know. He says God already knows. You wonder what God thinks.

The meaning of life. The wasted years of life. The poor choices of life. God answers the mess of life with one word: *grace*.

We talk as though we understand the term. The bank gives us a *grace* period. The seedy politician falls from *grace*. Musicians speak of a *grace* note. We describe an actress as *gracious*, a dancer as *graceful*. We use the word for hospitals, baby girls, kings, and premeal prayers.

We talk as though we know what *grace* means.

Especially at church. *Grace* graces the songs we sing and the Bible verses we read. *Grace* shares the church parsonage with its cousins: *forgiveness*, *faith*, and *fellowship*. Preachers explain it. Hymns proclaim it. Seminaries teach it.

But do we really understand it?

Here's my hunch: we've settled for wimpy grace. It politely occupies a phrase in a hymn, fits nicely on a church sign. Never causes trouble or demands a response. When asked, "Do you believe in grace?" who could say no?

This book asks a deeper question: Have you been changed by grace? Shaped by grace? Strengthened by grace? Emboldened by grace? Softened by grace?

Snatched by the nape of your neck and shaken to your senses by grace? God's grace has a drenching about it. A wildness about it. A white-water, riptide, turn-you-upside-downness about it. Grace comes after you. It rewires you. From insecure to God secure. From regret-riddled to better-because-of-it. From afraid-to-die to ready-to-fly. Grace is the voice that calls us to change and then gives us the power to pull it off.[1]

When grace happens, we receive not a nice compliment from God but a new heart. Give your heart to Christ, and he returns the favor. "I will give you a new heart and put a new spirit within you" (Ezek. 36:26).[2]

You might call it a spiritual heart transplant.

———

Tara Storch understands this miracle as much as anyone can. In the spring of 2010 a skiing accident took the life of her thirteen-year-old daughter, Taylor. What followed for Tara and her husband, Todd, was every parent's worst nightmare: a funeral, a burial, a flood of questions and tears. They decided to donate their daughter's organs to needy patients. Few people needed a heart more than Patricia Winters. Her heart had begun to fail five years earlier, leaving her too weak to do much more than sleep. Taylor's heart gave Patricia a fresh start on life.

Tara had only one request: she wanted to hear the heart of her daughter. She and Todd flew from Dallas to Phoenix and went to Patricia's home to listen to Taylor's heart.

The two mothers embraced for a long time. Then Patricia offered Tara and Todd a stethoscope.[3] When they listened to the healthy rhythm, whose heart did they hear? Did they not hear the still-beating heart of their daughter? It indwells a different body, but the heart is the heart of their child. And when God hears your heart, does he not hear the still-beating heart of his Son?

As Paul said, "It is no longer I who live, but Christ lives in me" (Gal. 2:20). The apostle sensed within himself not just the philosophy, ideals, or influence of Christ but the person of Jesus. Christ moved in. He still does. When grace happens, Christ enters. "Christ in you, the hope of glory" (Col. 1:27).

For many years I missed this truth. I

believed all the other prepositions: Christ *for* me, *with* me, *ahead of* me. And I knew I was working *beside* Christ, *under* Christ, *with* Christ. But I never imagined that Christ was *in* me.

I can't blame my deficiency on Scripture. Paul refers to this union 216 times. John mentions it 26.[4] They describe a Christ who not only woos us to himself but "ones" us to himself. "Whoever confesses that Jesus is the Son of God, *God abides in him*, and he in God" (1 John 4:15, emphasis mine).

No other religion or philosophy makes such a claim. No other movement implies the living presence of its founder *in* his followers. Muhammad does not indwell Muslims. Buddha does not inhabit Buddhists. Hugh Hefner does not inhabit

SHAPED BY GRACE

the pleasure-seeking hedonist. Influence?
Instruct? Entice? Yes. But occupy? No.

Yet Christians embrace this
inscrutable promise. "The mystery in a
nutshell is just this: Christ is in you" (Col.
1:27 MSG). The Christian is a person in
whom Christ is happening.

We are Jesus Christ's; we belong to
him. But even more, we are *increasingly*
him. He moves in and commandeers our
hands and feet, requisitions our minds and
tongues. We sense his rearranging: debris
into the divine, pig's ear into silk purse.
He repurposes bad decisions and squalid
choices. Little by little a new image
emerges. "He decided from the outset
to shape the lives of those who love him
along the same lines as the life of his Son"
(Rom. 8:29 MSG).

Grace is God as heart surgeon, cracking open your chest, removing your heart—poisoned as it is with pride and pain—and replacing it with his own. Rather than tell you to change, he creates the change. Do you clean up so he can accept you? No, he accepts you and begins cleaning you up. His dream isn't just to get you into heaven but to get heaven into you. What a difference this makes! Can't forgive your enemy? Can't face tomorrow? Can't forgive your past? Christ can, and he is on the move, aggressively budging you from graceless to grace-shaped living. The gift-given giving gifts. Forgiven people forgiving people. Deep sighs of relief. Stumbles aplenty but despair seldom.

Grace is everything Jesus. Grace lives because he does, works because he works,

and matters because he matters. He placed
a term limit on sin and danced a victory
jig in a graveyard. To be saved by grace
is to be saved by him—not by an idea,
doctrine, creed, or church membership,
but by Jesus himself, who will sweep into
heaven anyone who so much as gives him
the nod.

Not in response to a finger snap,
religious chant, or a secret handshake.
Grace won't be stage-managed. I have no
tips on how to *get* grace. Truth is, we don't
get grace. But it sure can get us. Grace
hugged the stink out of the prodigal and
scared the hate out of Paul and pledges to
do the same in us.

If you fear you've written too many
checks on God's kindness account, drag
regrets around like a broken bumper, huff

and puff more than you delight and rest,
and, most of all, if you wonder whether
God can do something with the mess of
your life, then grace is what you need.

Let's make certain it happens to you.

CHAPTER 2

THE GRACE-SHAPED LIFE

The voices yanked her out of bed.

"Get up, you harlot."

"What kind of woman do you think you are?"

Priests slammed open the bedroom door, threw back the window curtains, and pulled off the covers. Before she felt the warmth of the morning sun, she felt the heat of their scorn.

"Shame on you."

"Pathetic."

"Disgusting."

She scarcely had time to cover her body before they marched her through the narrow streets. Dogs yelped. Roosters ran. Women leaned out their windows. Mothers snatched children off the path. Merchants peered out the doors of their shops. Jerusalem became a jury and rendered its verdict with glares and crossed arms.

And as if the bedroom raid and parade of shame were inadequate, the men thrust her into the middle of a morning Bible class.

> Early the next morning [Jesus] was back again at the Temple. A crowd soon gathered, and he sat down and taught them. As he was speaking, the teachers of religious law and Pharisees brought a woman they had caught in the act of adultery. They put her in front of the crowd.
>
> "Teacher," they said to Jesus, "this woman was caught in the very act of adultery. The law of Moses says to stone her. What do you say?" (John 8:2–5 NLT)

Stunned students stood on one side of her. Pious plaintiffs on the other. They had their questions and convictions; she had her dangling negligee and smeared lipstick. "This woman was caught in the very act of adultery," her accusers crowed. Caught in the *very* act. In the moment. In the arms. In the passion. Caught in the very act by the Jerusalem Council on Decency and Conduct. "The law of Moses says to stone her. What do you say?"

The woman had no exit. Deny the accusation? She had been caught. Plead for mercy? From whom? From God? His spokesmen were squeezing stones and snarling their lips. No one would speak for her.

But someone would stoop for her.

Jesus "stooped down and wrote in the

dust" (v. 6 NLT). We would expect him
to stand up, step forward, or even ascend
a stair and speak. But instead he leaned
over. He descended lower than anyone
else—beneath the priests, the people, even
beneath the woman. The accusers looked
down on her. To see Jesus, they had to
look down even farther.

He's prone to stoop. He stooped to
wash feet, to embrace children. Stooped
to pull Peter out of the sea, to pray in the
Garden. He stooped before the Roman
whipping post. Stooped to carry the
cross. Grace is a God who stoops. Here he
stooped to write in the dust.

Remember the first occasion his
fingers touched dirt? He scooped soil and
formed Adam. As he touched the sun-
baked soil beside the woman, Jesus may

have been reliving the creation moment, reminding himself from whence we came. Earthly humans are prone to do earthy things. Maybe Jesus wrote in the soil for his own benefit.

Or for hers? To divert gaping eyes from the scantily clad, just-caught woman who stood in the center of the circle?

The posse grew impatient with the silent, stooping Jesus. "They kept demanding an answer, so he stood up" (v. 7 NLT).

He lifted himself erect until his shoulders were straight and his head was high. He stood, not to preach, for his words would be few. Not for long, for he would soon stoop again. Not to instruct his followers; he didn't address them. He stood on behalf of the woman. He placed himself between her and the lynch mob and said, "'All right, stone her. But let those who have never sinned throw the first stones!' Then he stooped down again and wrote in the dust" (vv. 7–8 NLT).

Name-callers shut their mouths. Rocks fell to the ground. Jesus resumed his scribbling. "When the accusers heard this, they slipped away one by one, beginning with the oldest, until only Jesus was left in the middle of the crowd with the woman" (v. 9 NLT).

Jesus wasn't finished. He stood one final time and asked the woman, "Where are your accusers?" (v. 10 NLT).

My, my, my. What a question—not just for her but for us. Voices of condemnation awaken us as well.

"You aren't good enough."

"You'll never improve."

"You failed—again."

The voices in our world.

And the voices in our heads! Who is this morality patrolman who issues a citation at every stumble? Who reminds us of every mistake? Does he ever shut up?

No. Because Satan never shuts up. The apostle John called him the Accuser: "This great dragon—the ancient serpent called the Devil, or Satan, the one deceiving the whole world—was thrown down to the earth with all his angels. Then I heard a loud voice shouting across the heavens, '. . . For the Accuser has been thrown down to earth—the one who accused our brothers and sisters before our God day and night'" (Rev. 12:9–10 NLT).

Day after day, hour after hour.

Relentless, tireless. The Accuser makes
a career out of accusing. Unlike the
conviction of the Holy Spirit, Satan's
condemnation brings no repentance or
resolve, just regret. He has one aim: "to
steal, and to kill, and to destroy" (John
10:10). Steal your peace, kill your dreams,
and destroy your future. He has deputized
a horde of silver-tongued demons to
help him. He enlists people to peddle
his poison. Friends dredge up your past.
Preachers proclaim all guilt and no grace.
And parents, oh, your parents. They own
a travel agency that specializes in guilt
trips. They distribute it twenty-four hours
a day. Long into adulthood you still hear
their voices: "Why can't you grow up?"
"When are you going to make me proud?"

Condemnation—the preferred

commodity of Satan. He will repeat the adulterous woman scenario as often as you permit him to do so, marching you through the city streets and dragging your name through the mud. He pushes you into the center of the crowd and megaphones your sin:

This person was caught in the act of immorality . . . stupidity . . . dishonesty . . . irresponsibility.

But he will not have the last word. Jesus has acted on your behalf.

He stooped. Low enough to sleep in a manger, work in a carpentry shop, sleep in a fishing boat. Low enough to rub shoulders with crooks and lepers. Low enough to be spat upon, slapped, nailed,

and speared. Low. Low enough to be
buried.

And then he stood. Up from the
slab of death. Upright in Joseph's tomb
and right in Satan's face. Tall. High. He
stood up for the woman and silenced her
accusers, and he does the same for you.

He "is in the presence of God at this
very moment sticking up for us" (Rom.
8:34 MSG). Let this sink in for a moment.
In the presence of God, in defiance of
Satan, Jesus Christ rises to your defense.
He takes on the role of a priest. "Since we
have a great priest over God's house, let
us come near to God with a sincere heart
and a sure faith, because we have been
made free from a guilty conscience" (Heb.
10:21–22 NCV).

A clean conscience. A clean record.

A clean heart. Free from accusation. Free from condemnation. Not just for our past mistakes but also for our future ones.

"Since he will live forever, he will always be there to remind God that he has paid for [our] sins with his blood" (Heb. 7:25 TLB). Christ offers unending intercession on your behalf.

Jesus trumps the devil's guilt with words of grace.

> Though we were spiritually dead
> because of the things we did against
> God, he gave us new life with Christ.
> You have been saved by God's grace.
> And he raised us up with Christ
> and gave us a seat with him in the
> heavens. He did this for those in
> Christ Jesus so that for all future time

he could show the very great riches of his grace by being kind to us in Christ Jesus. I mean that you have been saved by grace through believing. You did not save yourselves; it was a gift from God. It was not the result of your own efforts, so you cannot brag about it. God has made us what we are. In Christ Jesus, God made us to do good works, which God planned in advance for us to live our lives doing. (Eph. 2:5–10 NCV)

Behold the fruit of grace: saved by God, raised by God, seated with God. Gifted, equipped, and commissioned. Farewell, earthly condemnations: *Stupid. Unproductive. Slow learner. Fast talker. Quitter. Cheapskate.* No longer. You are who *he* says you are: *Spiritually alive. Heavenly positioned. Connected to God. A billboard of mercy. An honored child.* This is the "aggressive forgiveness we call grace" (Rom. 5:20 MSG).

Satan is left speechless and without ammunition.

> Who can accuse the people God has chosen? No one, because God is the One who makes them right. Who can say God's people are guilty? No one, because Christ Jesus died, but he was also raised from the dead, and now he is on God's right side, appealing to God for us. (Rom. 8:33–34 NCV).

The accusations of Satan sputter and fall like a deflated balloon.

Then why, pray tell, do we still hear them? Why do we, as Christians, still feel guilt?

Not all guilt is bad. God uses appropriate doses of guilt to awaken us to sin. We know guilt is God given when it causes "indignation . . . alarm . . . longing . . . concern . . . readiness to see justice done" (2 Cor. 7:11 NIV). God's guilt brings enough regret to change us.

Satan's guilt, on the other hand, brings enough regret to enslave us. Don't let him lock his shackles on you.

Remember, "your life is hidden with Christ in God" (Col. 3:3). When he looks at you, he sees Jesus first. In the Chinese language the word for *righteousness* is a combination of two characters, the figure of a lamb and a person. The lamb is on top, covering the person. Whenever God looks down at you, this is what he sees: the perfect Lamb of God covering you. It boils down to this choice: Do you trust your Advocate or your Accuser?

Your answer has serious implications. It did for Jean Valjean. Victor Hugo introduced us to this character in the classic *Les Misérables*. Valjean enters the pages as a vagabond. A just-released prisoner in midlife, wearing threadbare trousers and a tattered jacket. Nineteen years in a French prison have left him rough and fearless. He's walked for four days in the Alpine chill of nineteenth-century southeastern France, only to find that no inn will take him, no tavern will feed him. Finally he knocks on the door of a bishop's house.

———

Monseigneur Myriel is seventy-five years old. Like Valjean, he has lost much. The revolution took all the valuables from his family except some silverware, a soup ladle, and two candlesticks. Valjean tells his story and expects the religious man to turn him away. But the bishop is kind. He asks the visitor to sit near a fire. "You did not need to tell me who you were," he explains. "This is not my house—it is the house of Jesus Christ."[1] After some time the bishop takes the ex-convict to the table, where they dine on soup and bread, figs, and cheese with wine, using the bishop's fine silverware.

He shows Valjean to a bedroom. In spite of the comfort, the ex-prisoner can't sleep. In spite of the kindness of the bishop, he can't resist the temptation. He stuffs the silverware into his knapsack. The priest sleeps through the robbery, and Valjean runs into the night.

But he doesn't get far. The policemen catch him and march him back to the bishop's house. Valjean knows what his capture means—prison for the rest of his life. But then something wonderful happens. Before the officer can explain the crime, the bishop steps forward.

"Oh! Here you are! I'm so glad to see you. I can't believe you forgot the candlesticks! They are made of pure silver as well . . . Please take them with the forks and spoons I gave you."

Valjean is stunned. The bishop dismisses the policemen and then turns and says, "Jean Valjean, my brother, you no longer belong to evil, but to good. I

———

have bought your soul from you. I take it back from evil thoughts and deeds and the Spirit of Hell, and I give it to God."[2]

Valjean has a choice: believe the priest or believe his past. Jean Valjean believes the priest. He becomes the mayor of a small town. He builds a factory and gives jobs to the poor. He takes pity on a dying mother and raises her daughter.

Grace changed him. Let it change you. Give no heed to Satan's voice. You "have an Advocate with the Father, Jesus Christ the righteous" (1 John 2:1). As your Advocate, he defends you and says on your behalf, "There is therefore now no condemnation to those who are in Christ Jesus" (Rom. 8:1). Take that, Satan!

Wasn't this the message of Jesus to the woman?

"Where are your accusers? Didn't even one of them condemn you?"

"No, Lord," she said.

And Jesus said, "Neither do I. Go and sin no more." (John 8:10–11 NLT)

Within a few moments the courtyard was empty. Jesus, the woman, her critics—they all left. But let's linger. Look at the rocks on the ground, abandoned and unused. And look at the scribbling in the dust. It's the only sermon Jesus ever wrote. Even though we don't know the words, I'm wondering if they read like this:

"Grace happens here."

CHAPTER 3

THE SHAPE OF GRACE

Trapped beneath two thousand feet of solid rock, thirty-three Chilean miners were desperate. The collapse of a main tunnel had sealed their exit and thrust them into survival mode. They ate two spoonfuls of tuna, a sip of milk, and a morsel of peaches—every other day. For two months they prayed for someone to save them.

On the surface above, the Chilean rescue team worked around the clock, consulting NASA, meeting with experts. They designed a thirteen-foot-tall capsule and drilled, first a communication hole, then an excavation tunnel. There was no guarantee of success. No one had ever been trapped underground this long and lived to tell about it.

Now someone has.

On October 13, 2010, the men began to emerge, slapping high fives and leading victory chants. A great-grandfather. A forty-four-year-old who was planning a wedding. Then a nineteen-year-old. All had different stories, but all had made the same decision. They trusted someone else to save them. No one returned the rescue offer with a declaration of independence: "I can get out of here on my own. Just give me a new drill." They had stared at the stone tomb long enough to reach the unanimous opinion: "We need help. We need someone to penetrate this world and pull us out." And when the rescue capsule came, they climbed in.

Would you do the same? Climb into the capsule of grace. Let God pull you out. Trust in his strength. It's as easy as A-B-C.

Admit. Admit your wrongdoing. Admit that you are a sinner in need of a Savior.

Believe. Believe that Jesus is who he says he is. The Savior of the world. Believe he did what the Bible says he did. He died for your sins and mine. He vacated the grave and he reigns as Lord over the world.

Commit. Commit your life to his cause. Confess your belief privately and publicly. Find a church where you can be baptized and grow in your faith.

There is no fine print. A second shoe is not going to drop. God's promise has no hidden language. Let grace happen, for heaven's sake. Of all the things you must earn in life, God's unending affection is not one of them. You have it. Stretch yourself out in the hammock of grace.

Would you let him save you? This is the most important decision you will ever make. Why don't you give your heart to him right now? Go to God in prayer and tell him, *I am a sinner in need of grace. I believe that Jesus died for me on the cross. I accept your offer of salvation.*

It's a simple prayer with eternal results.

YOUR
RESPONSE

I believe that Jesus Christ is the Son of the living God. I want him to be the Lord of my life.

Chelsea Norris
Signed

07-06-13
Date

NOTES

CHAPTER 1: THE GRACE-SHAPED HEART

1. My late friend Tim Hansel said something
   similar in his book *You Gotta Keep Dancin'*
   (Elgin, IL: David C. Cook Publishing Co.,
   1985), 107.
2. Also see John 14:20; Romans 8:10;
   Galatians 2:20.
3. Todd and Tara Storch, parents of Taylor and
   founders of Taylor's Gift Foundation (www
   .TaylorsGift.org), tell the ongoing story
   of their journey of regifting life, renewing
   health, and restoring families in their book
   *Taylor's Gift: A Courageous Story of Life,
   Loss, and Unexpected Blessings* (with Jennifer
   Schuchmann, forthcoming in 2013 from

Revell Books, a division of Baker Publishing
Group).

4. Bruce Demarest, *The Cross and Salvation:
The Doctrine of Salvation* (Wheaton, IL:
Crossway Books, 1997), 289.

CHAPTER 2: THE GRACE-SHAPED LIFE

1. Jim Reimann, *Victor Hugo's Les Misérables*
(Nashville: Word Publishing, 2001), 16.
2. Ibid., 29–31.

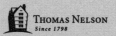

Tools for Your Church or Small Group

GRACE DVD-Based Study
978-1-4016-7582-0 | $39.99

Join Max Lucado through seven DVD sessions ideal for small-group settings.

GRACE Participant's Guide
978-1-4016-7584-4 | $9.99

Filled with Scripture study, discussion questions, and practical ideas designed to lead group members to a deeper understanding and application of grace, this guide is an integral part of the *GRACE* small-group study.

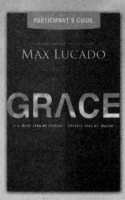

Grace for Every Age

Grace for the Moment: 365 Devotions for Kids
978-1-4003-2034-9 | $15.99

Adapted from the best-selling devotional for adults, *Grace for the Moment: 365 Devotions for Kids* presents the message of God's grace in a way that children can easily under-stand, perfect for families to read together or for older readers to enjoy alone.

Wild Grace
978-1-4003-2084-4 | $14.99

This adaptation of *GRACE* shows teens—no matter how messed up, off track, or in trouble they may be—grace can change their lives in powerful ways.

Inspired by what you just read?
Connect with Max.

Listen to Max's teaching ministry, UpWords,
on the radio and online.
Visit www.MaxLucado.com to get FREE resources for
spiritual growth and encouragement, including:

- Archives of UpWords, Max's daily radio program,
  and a list of radio stations where it airs
- Devotionals and e-mails from Max
- First look at book excerpts
- Downloads of audio, video, and printed
  material
- Mobile content

You will also find an online store and special offers.

www.MaxLucado.com

1-800-822-9673

UpWords Ministries
P.O. Box 692170
San Antonio, TX 78269-2170

Join the Max Lucado community:

Follow Max on Twitter @MaxLucado
or at Facebook.com/UpWordsMinistry